Fact Finders®

TechSafetySmarts

Gaming Safely

by Allyson Valentine Schrier

Consultant:
Frank W. Baker
Media Literacy Consultant
Media Literacy Clearinghouse Inc.

CAPSTONE PRESS
a capstone imprint

Fact Finders are published by Capstone Press,
1710 Roe Crest Drive, North Mankato, Minnesota 56003
www.capstonepub.com

Library of Congress Cataloging-in-Publication Data
Schrier, Allyson Valentine.
Gaming safely / by Allyson Valentine Schrier.
p. cm.—(Fact finders. Tech safety smarts.)
Includes bibliographical references and index.
Summary: "Describes safe online gaming and ways to avoid dangerous situations, such as identity theft, cyberbullying, or predators"—Provided by publisher.
ISBN 978-1-4296-9946-4 (library binding) — ISBN 978-1-62065-800-0 (pbk.)
ISBN 978-1-4765-1574-8 (eBook PDF)
1. Internet games—Juvenile literature. 2. Internet—Safety measures—Juvenile literature. I. Title.
GV1469.15.S35 2013
794.8′2—dc23 2012029268

Editorial Credits
Jennifer Besel, editor; Sarah Bennett, designer; Laura Manthe, production specialist

Photo Credits
iStockphotos: Cruz Puga, 26, Kamruzzaman Ratan, 20, Lee Daniels, 11, liangpv, 7, Louis-Paul St-Onge, 6, Matthew Cole, 12-13, Vetta/ryccio, 28; Shutterstock: Atelier Sommerland, 14 (inset), AVAVA, 25, Catmando, 17, diversepixel, 4, DM7, 4 (robot), Eka Panova, 12 (monkey), 13 (mouse), freelanceartist, 10, Gigra, 5, greglith, 15 (robot), Jens Stolt, 23 (rhino), Master3D, 19 (road), Maxx-Studio, 23 (drum), mkabakov, 24 (bottom), Nyuuness, 8, Phil Date, 29, ponsuwan, 19 (traffic light), Portfolio, cover (gamepad), Redshinestudio, 22, Smit, 23 (pizza), Unholy Vault Designs, 14, VLADGRIN, cover (icons), VLADJ55, 16-17, zhnag kan, 24 (top); The ESRB rating icons are registered trademarks of the Entertainment Software Association, Rating images courtesy of ESRB, 15

Artistic Effects
iStockphotos: alengo, Bennyart, file404, John T Takai, kentoh, LongQuattro, Merydolla, Mikhail, nrt, SoooInce, VikaSuh, VLADGRIN

Printed in the United States of America in North Mankato, Minnesota.
112018 001249

Table of Contents

Power up, Gamer

You're online playing your favorite game. Suddenly a new character appears. A message pops up on your screen. "Hey! I've been on this quest before. Give me your cell number, and I'll text you some tips."

You're about to start typing your number. But then you think twice.

Should you respond if you don't know who you're writing to?

For many kids, online computer games are a favorite activity. And with friends just a mouse click away, you never have to play alone. The trouble is that you and your friends aren't the only ones playing. Millions of people around the world are online too. Playing an online game is like being in a room with millions of people who are all wearing masks. You can never be totally sure who anyone really is. Online gaming can be tons of fun. But playing online comes with a big responsibility.

Talk about It

Throughout this book, you'll find "Talk about It" boxes that set up real-life situations you might run into. Use these boxes as discussion starters at home or at school. Talk about the pros and cons of different actions, and decide how you could stay safe in each situation.

So, should you respond to a message in a game from someone you don't know?

Your Responsibility

When you're playing online, it's your job to keep yourself safe. Gaming is a great way to connect with friends. But gaming online is not all fun. You can run into unsafe people and situations. Consider the situation on the previous pages. Would you give your phone number to a stranger in a game?

If you're not sure what to do, think about what you'd do if you met a stranger on the street. Would you give private information to him or her then? No way! Then you shouldn't give it out in a game either.

Remember that your online life is part of your real life. Only you have the power to keep your online gaming fun and safe.

Sticky Situations

A kid with a super cool **avatar** invites you to join him in a quest online. You make a terrific team! You agree to meet again the next night, same time. A few more online battles together, and it feels as if you're old friends. But are you really friends?

avatar—an electronic identity that represents a computer user

The answer to that question is yes and no. Yes, you are online friends. But you are not offline friends. And that's a big difference. You can be sure offline friends are who they say they are. You can see their facial expressions. You know they're not wearing a mask. But you can't do that with online friends. People on the other end could send fake pictures or lie about their age. And you wouldn't know.

Chances are good that online friends are nice people. But as an online gamer, you have to know the risks. The Federal Bureau of Investigation (FBI) says there are about 250,000 adults online every day who are looking to hurt kids. These people try to trick kids into being their friends. They say nice things about a kid's character and offer in-game gifts. Over time they begin asking for private information. Some of these dangerous adults try to meet kids in real life so they can hurt them.

Bullies

Researchers say that six out of 10 kids have had a bad experience online. A "bad experience" could include downloading **viruses** or being approached by dangerous people. It also includes being **cyberbullied**.

Cyberbullying is a growing problem online, especially in games. Massively Multiplayer Online games (MMOs) are played by millions of people at the same time. That's one giant playground! And it's a lot like the playground at school. Sure you can have tons of fun and hang out with friends. But you might also run into cyberbullies who lie, steal, or cheat.

SIX out of **TEN** kids have had a bad online experience.

virus—a computer program that is hidden in another program in order to harm a computer

cyberbully—to spread mean messages, rumors, or threats using technology

Cyberbullies in a game might send mean messages or try to harm your character. If you are bothered by a bully, resist the urge to fight back. But you don't have to put up with cyberbullies! Here are some things you can do.

- Use in-game settings to block the bully from contacting you.
- Turn off the game's chat option.
- Switch to another server if the game allows that.
- Report the bully to the game supervisor. This person can block the bully from the game.
- Definitely let your parents or trusted adults know what's going on. They will have other ideas on how to handle the situation.

Popping Up

There you are, shampooing your virtual pet. Suddenly a box pops onto the screen, telling you to "click here" to win a prize.

Is there a prize? Probably not. Most likely, the pop-up was put there by someone trying to sell you something. But some pop-ups are worse than that. Some pop-ups spread computer viruses. Sometimes "clicking here" takes you to an inappropriate site that was not meant for kids.

Protect yourself, and don't take the bait! If you can, simply close the pop-up. But if you're stuck someplace you didn't mean to go, ask an adult for help right away.

Parents and Trusted Adults

When you're gaming, there are many things you can do to keep yourself safe. But sometimes situations come up that you can't control. Don't hesitate to talk to your parents or other trusted adults about anything that happens in a game.

Talking to adults isn't always easy. It can be embarrassing or even scary to tell them what's going on. But know that they care and want to help you stay safe. So talk to them!

In the News

Police officers in the Utah Internet Crimes Against Children Task Force keep online **predators** *from hurting kids. The officers pose as kids playing online games. Predators are convinced that the officers are regular kids—and possible victims. The predators invite the disguised officers to meet in the real world. When they meet, the officers are able to arrest the predators before any real kids get hurt.*

predator—a person who follows another person in order to hurt them in some way

Rated B for Beware

How do you pick which games to play? Maybe the most realistic **graphics** draw you in. Maybe it's the most action. Or do you choose the game that your friends are playing? No matter what you're looking for in a game, deciding what to play is an important decision. All games are not meant for everyone.

Online games for kids often have monitors who watch out for bullies. These games also don't allow inappropriate conversations and try to protect kids from dangerous people.

graphic—a visual image such as an illustration, photograph, or work of art

Games meant for older players have more realistic graphics and violence. They also deal with topics that are not kid-friendly.

So how do you find the safest games? Start by checking their ratings. You know movies rated G are clean and safe. Movies rated R are adult-only. Games have a similar rating system. The Entertainment Software Rating Board (ESRB) reviews and rates games. Look for game ratings on the ESRB website or on game packages. Games rated E are for everyone. An E10+ means the game is good for kids 10 years and older. Save games rated M for when you're at least 17.

The ESRB only looks at the game to make the ratings though. So you could still run into foul language in chats. But playing a game meant for kids your age makes it less likely you'll run into problems.

A Not-so-Freebie

Choosing a game to play can often come down to cost. Free games seem like a great idea when you're low on cash. But be careful with free games. Many free games are not rated by the ESRB. There's no way to know what or who you'll run into when you play.

Free games can turn out to be pretty expensive too. It may cost nothing to download a free game. But it could cost a lot to rid your computer of viruses that snuck in with it. And be aware of in-game items that cost real money. One gamer spent $300,000 of real money on an item in a virtual world!

Be careful to read what you're selecting in a game to see if it will cost real money. Then check with your parents or guardians before buying anything. If you're not careful, you could end up spending all your time doing chores to pay back the money spent on the online purchase.

Talk about it

You're playing a game and having trouble beating the wizard. Your friend says you'll need to buy a special sword to complete the quest.

What do you do?

Buckle up For Safety

Playing games online can be a bit risky. But that doesn't mean you have to stop. If you take steps to protect yourself, you'll be a safe and savvy gamer.

Start protecting yourself by safeguarding your information. There are two kinds of info—public and private. Public info is stuff you don't mind others knowing. Your favorite pizza topping or your fastest swim time are public info. Private info is stuff that belongs just to you. Your home address or **Social Security number** are things that could lead a dangerous person to you in real life. It's best to keep that kind of info secret from online (and offline) strangers.

Talk about It

While playing online you meet a kid who likes the game as much as you do. You start chatting. He's funny and nice. He asks for your address so he can come over to play.

What do you do?

Social Security number—an identification number that is assigned to only you

Green Means GO

Race through this quiz and stop at each traffic light. Decide which pieces of information are public and get the green light to share. What pieces of info should make you stop?

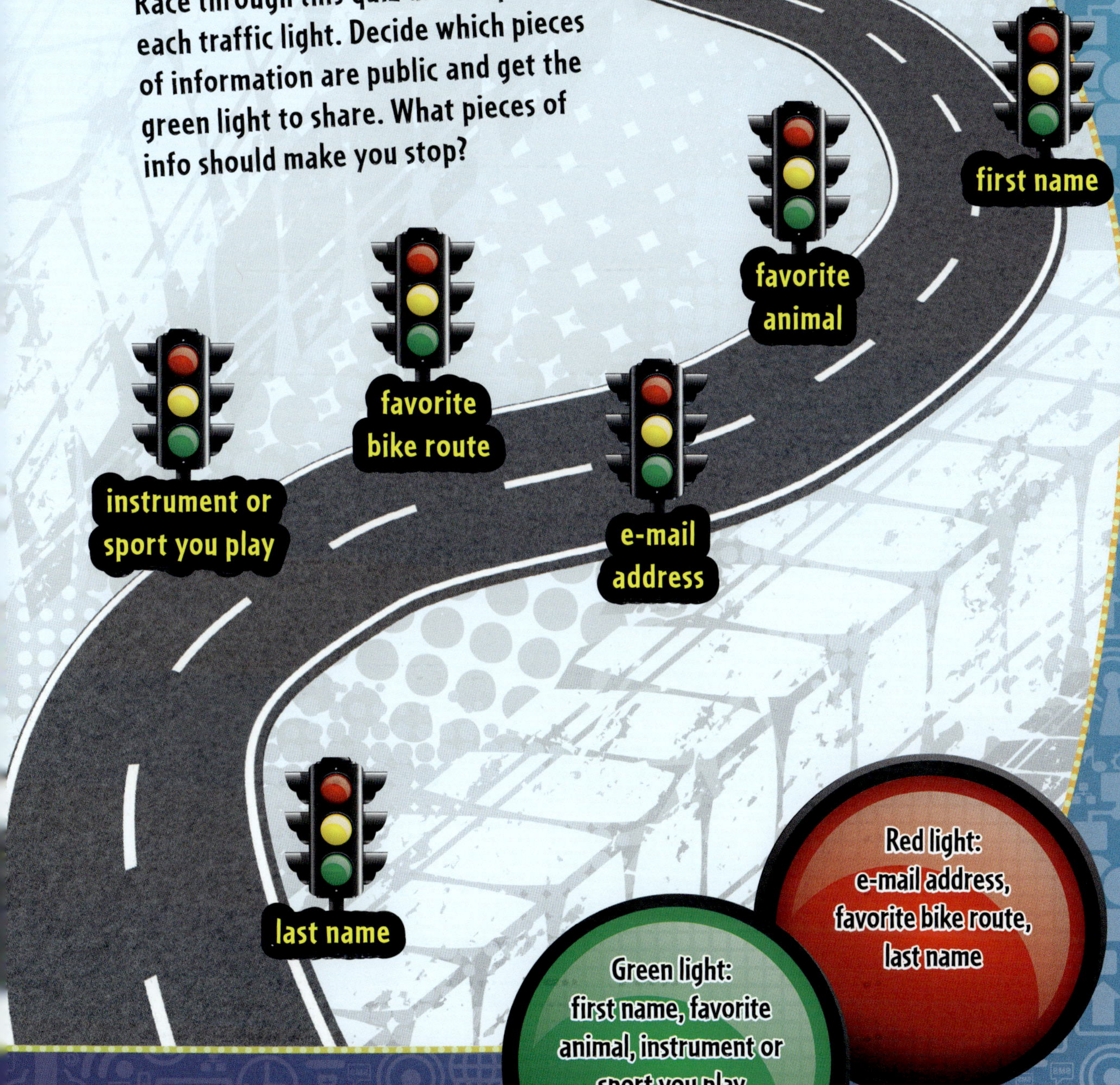

Green light:
first name, favorite animal, instrument or sport you play

Red light:
e-mail address, favorite bike route, last name

Talk It Up

It might seem as if there are a lot of off-limit topics. But there are plenty of things to talk about with online friends. You can talk about the books or TV shows you like. You can talk about the latest sports event. And, of course, you can always talk about the game! Share tips and strategies. Discuss ideas for winning a battle. Focus on in-game activities. After all, the game is what you're there for.

I Can See You

Using a live video option while gaming can give dangerous people details about you. With video, people can see your age, your gender, and possibly your location. These live options can make gaming more exciting. But they can also be a risk. Before using video gaming, talk with your parents or guardians. They can help you decide if it's a good idea.

In the News

Julia was 12 years old when she met an 18-year-old man in an online game. Soon he asked for her address and cell phone number. The two began **flirting** over the phone and through texts. The man told Julia he wanted to marry her. He then did his research. He found an airline that would allow the 12-year-old to fly without her parents' permission. He bought her a ticket, and she flew to meet him.

Julia's mother called the police. She told them about the boy from the game. Police went to the man's house and found him and Julia together. Luckily, the police arrived before anything happened to Julia. And the man was taken to jail.

**Julia's name is made up to protect her privacy, but the story is true.*

flirt—to act romantic in a playful way

What's in a Name?

Your online ID is the name you go by in a game. But if you're not careful, your online ID can tell strangers a lot about you. The best bet when choosing an online name? Go for neutral.

First make sure your online ID doesn't give out private information. Would the ID "trevorsmithage12" be a good choice? Nope. It gives out your full name and your age.

Also avoid an ID that might invite dangerous people to be your friend. Someone who likes to flirt with young girls would be more drawn to a player with the ID "Cutiepie" than to someone called "Gamer99." Get the idea?

So what does make a good ID name? For a fun ID that won't give away too much, try putting together two unrelated words.

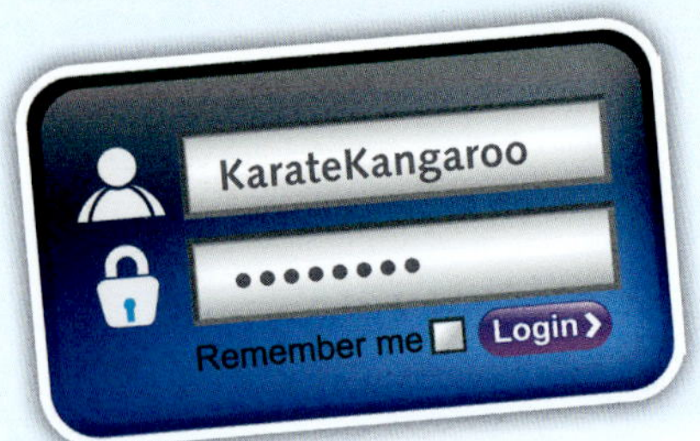

Talk about it

Your friend thought it would be funny to create an online avatar with the name "Hotchick."

What should you do?

Choose a topic from the blue column and think of your favorite thing in that category. Do the same with a topic from the green column. Then put the two words together for a crazy, funny online ID.

blue	green
sport	food
color	game
style of music	season
days of the week	type of vehicle
number	kind of insect
musical instrument	animal

How about "pizzadrum" for a funny online ID?

Maybe "greenrhino" would be a perfect online ID.

Lock It

Creating a strong password is an important safety measure too. An easy password could allow strangers to figure out how to login as you. If that happens, strangers could play as your character. They could break the rules of the game, getting you in trouble. Or they could send hurtful messages that look like you sent them.

The best passwords use a combination of capital and lowercase letters, numbers, and special characters. But complicated passwords can be hard to remember. So be creative! Come up with passwords that are easy for you to remember but hard for someone else to guess.

Weak Password	Strong Password
123456	youRgr8!
james1	Good2G0
123abc	1C00lkiD

Strong passwords won't do you any good if you share them. The only people who should know your passwords are your parents or guardians. Even your best friend could accidently pass them on to someone else. So keep passwords strong and secret, and you've done a lot to keep your online gaming safe.

STOP!

Answer these questions before you read any further in the book.

- Do you find yourself gaming for longer and longer periods of time?
- Do you lie about how much you play online games?
- Is it really hard to get the game out of your head?
- Do you get angry when your parents or guardians say it's time to stop playing?
- Are your homework or test scores suffering because you're too busy gaming to study?

If you said yes to any one of these, you might be playing more than you should. Said yes to two or more? It's time to talk with your parents or guardians. You need some help balancing game time and other parts of your life.

Even if you answered "no" to all those questions, it's still important to watch your gaming habits. Gaming is so much fun, it's easy to get wrapped up in it. Here are some safe, healthy gaming habits that can help.

Set limits

Work with your parents or guardians to make reasonable limits about when to play and for how long. Then set a timer that reminds you to shut off the game.

Choose nonaddictive games

Some games reward you for playing longer by giving you extra loot or levels. These tricks make it hard to stop playing. The best games allow you to stop without losing anything.

Balance exercise and gaming

An hour of exercise for an hour of screen time, perhaps? Or try exergames that are both fun and a great workout.

Winning the Battle

Staying safe in online games isn't much different from staying safe in real life. You already know how to protect yourself by steering clear of strangers. You know you should keep your parents or guardians in the loop about your activities. You also know that private information should stay secret.

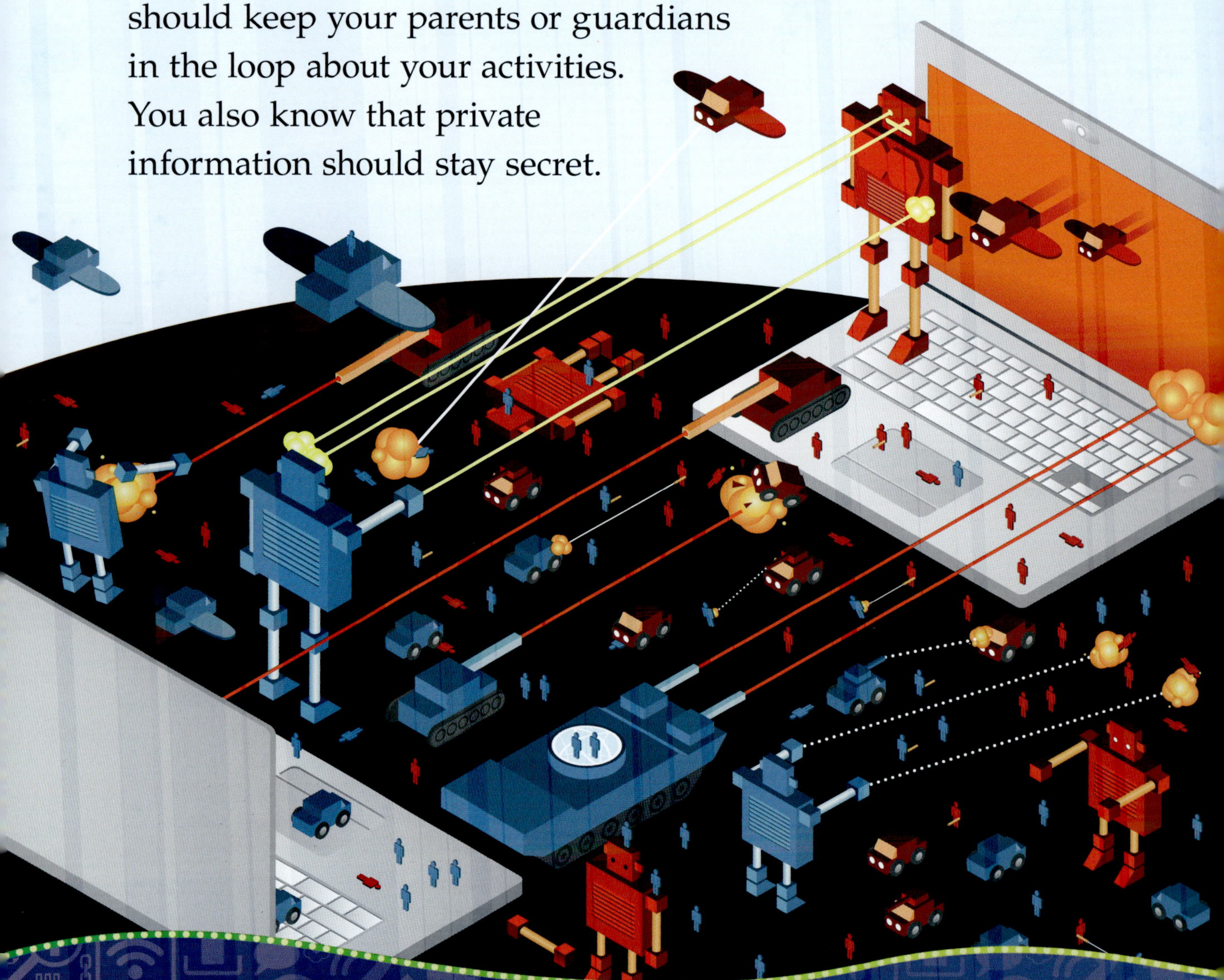

Of course, things are a little different online. It's easy to forget that a real person is behind that avatar. It's easy to find yourself in conversations with strangers. It's also easy to hide what you're doing from your parents or guardians.

Remember that when you're gaming, your safety is your responsibility. Be aware of what you're doing and who you're talking to. And if something feels wrong, get help right away. When you're safe, you'll find your time online is even more fun!

Glossary

avatar (AV-uh-tar)—an electronic identity that represents a computer user

cyberbully (SI-bur-buhl-ee)—to spread mean messages, rumors, or threats using technology

flirt (FLURT)—to act romantic in a playful way

graphic (GRA-fik)—a visual image such as an illustration, photograph, or work of art

predator (PRED-uh-tur)—a person who follows another person in order to hurt them

Social Security number (SOH-shul si-KYOOR-i-tee NUHM-bur)—an identification number that is assigned to only you; it is used to receive government benefits and is needed in order to get jobs, loans, or credit cards

virus (VYE-russ)—a computer program that is hidden in another program in order to harm a computer

Read More

Schwartz, Heather E. *Cyberbullying*. Tech Safety Smarts. Mankato, Minn.: Capstone Press, 2013.

Spivet, Bonnie. *Playing Games Online*. Cybersmarts: Staying Safe Online. New York.: PowerKids Press, 2012.

Wilkinson, Colin. *Gaming: Playing Safe and Playing Smart*. Digital and Information Literacy. New York: Rosen Central, 2012.

Internet Sites

FactHound offers a safe, fun way to find Internet sites related to this book. All of the sites on FactHound have been researched by our staff.

Here's all you do:

Visit *www.facthound.com*

Type in this code: 9781429699464

Index

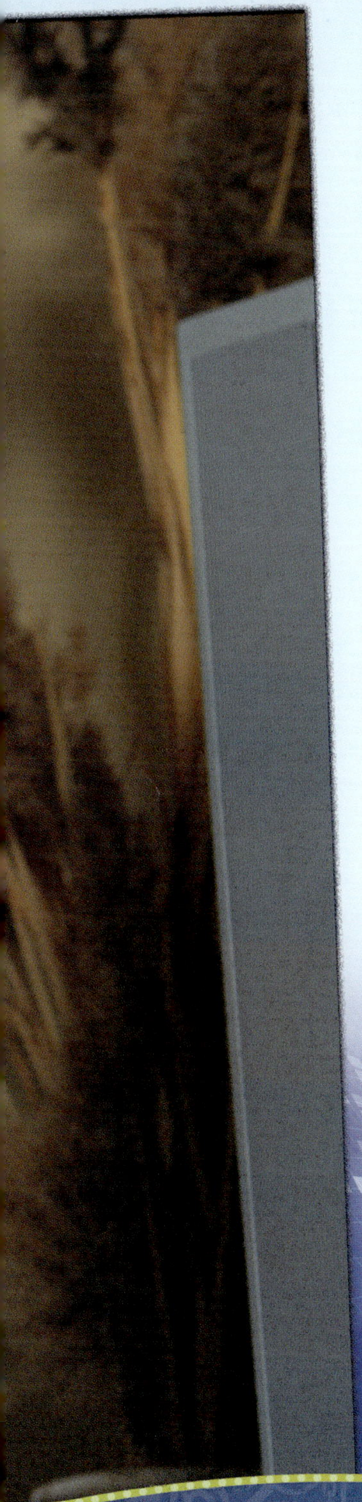

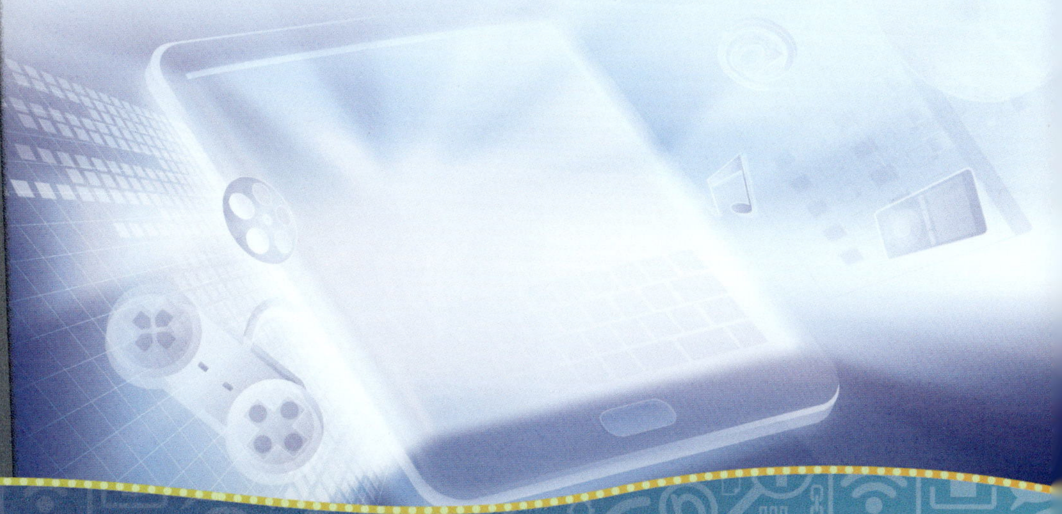

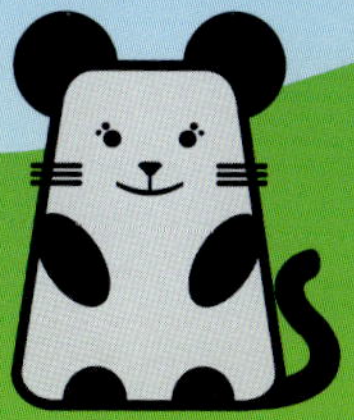

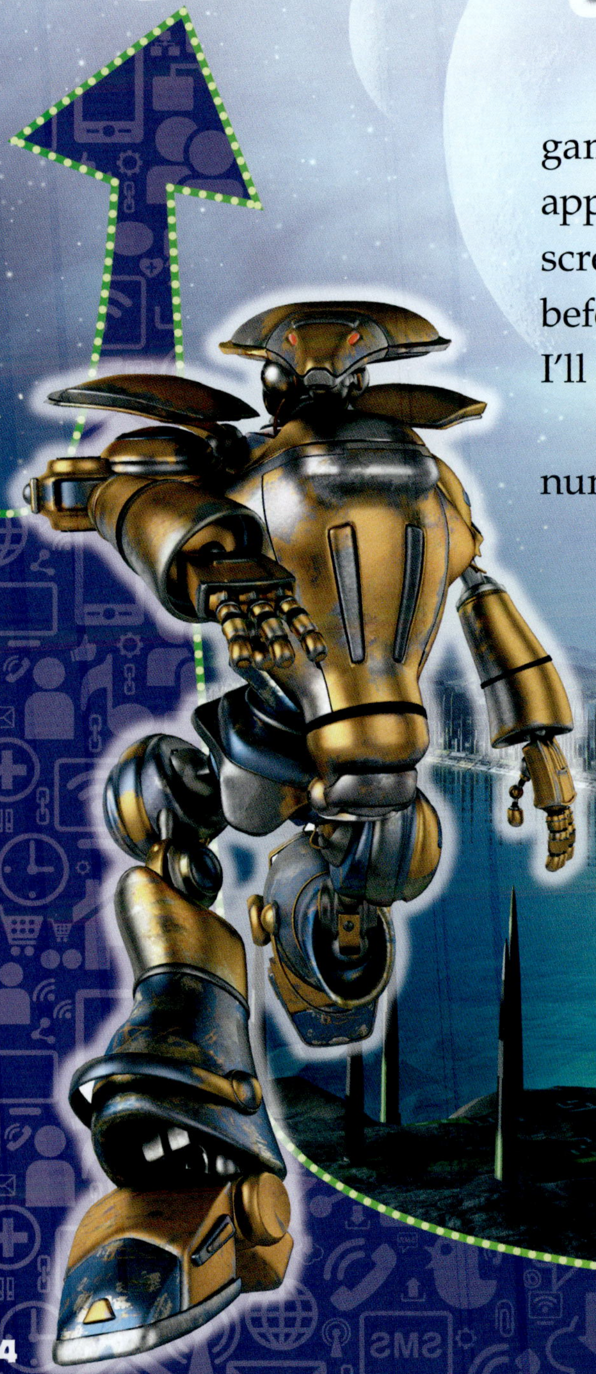

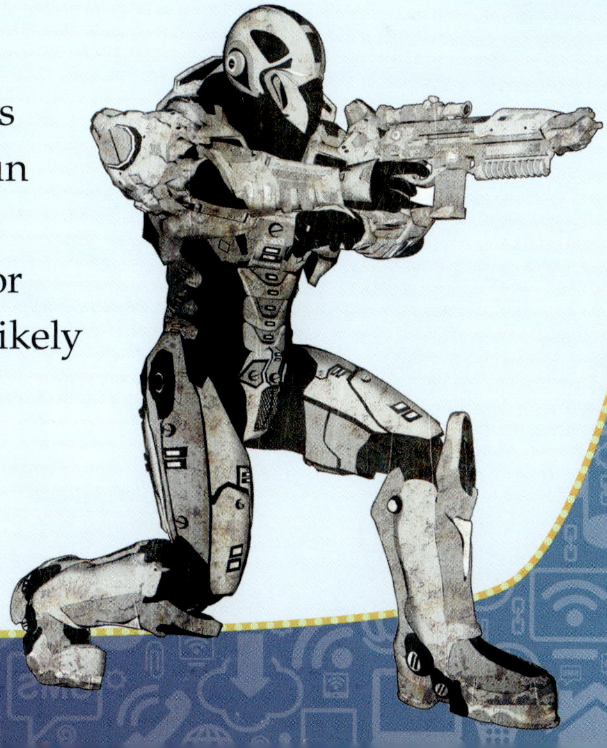

Green Means GO

Race through this quiz and stop at each traffic light. Decide which pieces of information are public and get the green light to share. What pieces of info should make you stop?

first name

favorite animal

e-mail address

favorite bike route

instrument or sport you play

last name

Red light:
e-mail address, favorite bike route, last name

Green light:
first name, favorite animal, instrument or sport you play

Index

If a strange character offers you a gift in an online game, do you know what to do?

Don't worry if you don't. This book is here to help!

Learn tech-savvy ways to keep your game sites safe—without taking away all the fun!

TechSafetySmarts

Using technology, such as a cell phone or social networking site, is a blast. But it can also open doors to unsafe situations. Protect yourself by getting all the facts on what to watch out for. Only you have the power to keep technology useful, safe, and fun.

Titles in this set:

Cell Phone Safety

Cyberbullying

Gaming Safely

Safe Social Networking

RL: 3-4 IL: 3-6

ISBN 978-1-62065-800-0

Capstone Press

a capstone imprint www.capstonepub.com

Gaming Safely

by Allyson Valentine Schrier

Fact Finders®

Index

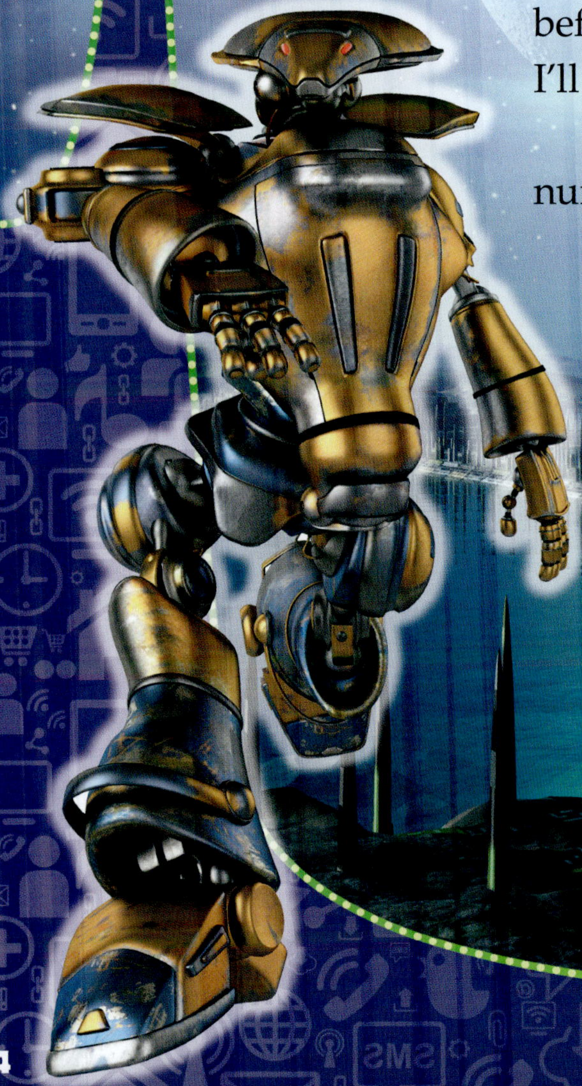

Index